# Dulwich Picture Gallery

**A Visitor's Guide by Desmond Shawe -Taylor**

# The Ernest Cook Trust

Ernest Cook, the grandson of Thomas Cook, who founded the Travel Agency, ran the family firm together with his brother Frank until they were of an age to retire. When they sold the business in 1928 Ernest's interests turned to art, to the patronage of which he devoted his fortune and remaining years. During the first ten years following his retirement Ernest Cook bought a large number of paintings; he also bought furniture, tapestries and porcelain, forming a collection which on his death in 1955 he bequeathed to the National Arts Collection Fund. It was, and remains, the largest single donation ever to have been made throughout England. Ernest Cook's passion for collecting broadened to include country houses and, later, the country estates in which they stood. They were bought simply to preserve them and, because as a bachelor he had few family obligations, they were bequeathed either to the National Trust or to the Ernest Cook Trust, which he founded in 1952 as an educational charity, endowing it with seven of his estates. Today ECT grants total some £500,000 a year. Because a substantial source of the Trust's income is the tenanted farms originally donated by the Trust's Founder emphasis is placed on educational work within the countryside, but Ernest Cook's interest in the arts has not been forgotten and the Trustees were pleased to support the production of this visitors' guide.

**Joseph Dakin** *Interior view of the Gallery, 1883*

# Dulwich College

The first player in the story of Dulwich Picture Gallery was Edward Alleyn (1566–1626). Alleyn and his rival, Richard Burbage (1573–1619), whose portrait also hangs in the Gallery, were the most celebrated actors on the Elizabethan stage. Their styles could not have been more different: Burbage was understated, Alleyn majestic and bombastic; Burbage was Shakespeare's favourite actor, Alleyn Christopher Marlowe's. Both, like Shakespeare, excelled in the business as well as the art of theatre: Alleyn amassed a considerable fortune, especially through his collaboration with his father-in-law, the impresario, Philip Henslowe. The precariously profitable world of the Elizabethan stage is brought to life in John Madden's 1998 film, *Shakespeare in Love*, in which all five characters mentioned above feature prominently.

In 1605 Edward Alleyn began to acquire his vast estates in Dulwich, still owned by the charity he founded, the College of God's Gift at Dulwich. The original Jacobean college, built by Alleyn in 1619, still stands next to the Gallery, though it has been much altered over the years. The actual school, Dulwich College, moved to new premises, some half a mile further along College Road, in 1870.

Edward Alleyn had a large collection of portraits, which were supplemented in 1686 by a bequest from another actor-manager, William Cartwright (1606–86). Until the the late nineteenth century, these paintings hung in a long Gallery in the Old College, to the right of figure 3.

British
School
*Edward
Alleyn*

British
School
*Richard
Burbage*

# The Bourgeois Bequest

One of the most successful art dealerships in London during the late eighteenth-century was the partnership of a Frenchman, Noël Desenfans (1745–1807), and his younger Swiss friend, the painter, Sir Francis Bourgeois, RA (1756–1811). The enterprise appears to have been launched by the dowry of Desenfans's Welsh wife, Margaret Morris (1737–1814). The three lived together in a house in Charlotte (now Hallam) Street, where they entertained with a well-heeled informality vividly evoked by Paul Sandby's small watercolour portrait.

The greatest moment in the career of the Bourgeois-Desenfans partnership came in 1790 when they were commissioned by Stanislaus Augustus, King of Poland, to form from scratch a Royal Collection in order to 'encourage the progress of the fine arts in Poland'. They devoted the next five years exclusively to this task, during which time Poland was gradually partitioned by its more powerful neighbours, leading in 1795 to its complete disappearance as an independent state. The King was forced to abdicate and the dealers were left with a Royal Collection on their hands.

Bourgeois and Desenfans recovered from this debacle in two ways. In private they sold individual works from

Attributed to Paul Sandby, *Bourgeois and Desenfans*. Watercolour

their Polish stock and replaced them with further important purchases. In public they sought a home for what they continued to call their 'Royal Collection', approaching amongst others the Tsar of Russia and the British Government. When it became obvious that they could not sell the collection in its entirety, they began to think to whom they might bequeath it, especially after Desenfans's death in 1807 when Bourgeois became sole owner. At that date there was no National Gallery, so the obvious candidate was the British Museum, but Bourgeois found its trustees too 'arbitrary' and 'aristocratic'. He decided to leave his collection to Dulwich College instead, though he had no obvious connection with the school. More important than the destination was the stipulation in the will that the paintings should be made available for the 'inspection of the public'.

So it was that Dulwich Picture Gallery – England's first public art gallery – was founded by the terms of Sir Francis Bourgeois's will upon his death in 1811.

'Taylor' *Dulwich College* 1796
Engraving, Dulwich College Archive

# Sir John Soane's Gallery Building

Bourgeois made another condition in his will: that the architect to be given the task of housing these paintings should be his friend, the most original designer of the period, Sir John Soane (1753–1837). The day after Bourgeois's death Soane was already on site thinking about what became, in the words of a friend, his 'favourite subject'. Soane's brief was not just to build a gallery but to redesign a college. Early ideas involved demolishing the two northern ranges and replacing them with three new ones to make up a complete new quadrangle. In the event there was only money for a single building, conceived as a new 'west wing for the college'. This wing performed three functions: it provided almshouses for six old ladies, display space for Bourgeois's collection of pictures and a Mausoleum for his mortal remains and those of his friends, Noël and Margaret Desenfans.

When it opened to the public in 1817 the Gallery had five display rooms, running the length of the east side of the building; to the west lay the almshouses and Mausoleum. Soane originally planned a covered walkway or *loggia* running across the east facade, a form often seen in English colleges. The actual loggia was abandoned for lack of money, but the same pattern of simple piers and arches was used in low relief to decorate the east facade.

**G Bailey**
(for John Soane)
*Dulwich College
and Gallery*
Pencil and
watercolour
Sir John Soane's
Museum

**J M Gandy**
*Mausoleum and
Picture Gallery with
God's Gift College
Dulwich*
Watercolour
Sir John Soane's
Museum

# Soane's Gallery Interior

The Soane building is probably the world's first purpose-built art gallery. This is a case of right first time. The famous sequence of arched spaces in Soane's interior (Rooms 1 to 5) is a shrine for Gallery designers, inspiring amongst many others Louis Kahn in his Kimball Art Museum, Robert Venturi at the Sainsbury Wing of the National Gallery in London and Richard Meyer at the new Getty Museum in Los Angeles. It is revered for practical and aesthetic reasons. Its roof-lanterns diffuse natural daylight, creating an even 'wash' of light over the walls, ideal for viewing paintings. The simple arches and smooth coved vaults provide interest without fuss. It is an architecture of harmonious lines rather than lavish decoration, and its elegant simplicity has never gone out of fashion.

**J M Gandy**
*Mausoleum and Picture Gallery with God's
Gift College Dulwich* (detail)
Watercolour
Sir John Soane's Museum

# The Bourgeois-Desenfans Mausoleum

The restrained practicality of the galleries contrasts with the theatrical brilliance of the Mausoleum. Thinking perhaps of the great chapels of Italy where art and death go hand in hand, Sir Francis Bourgeois decided to have himself and his co-founders, Noël and Margaret Desenfans, buried in their own gallery. The simple exterior of the Mausoleum is defined by square piers of brick with stone bases and cornices (a kind of 'almost-column' much used by Soane) and decorated with sarcophagi (antique-style stone coffins) with three closed doors to suggest a sealed vault.

Inside this confined area, Soane manages to stage a mini-drama of space and light. First we enter the chapel – a tiny circular temple in a square room, with primitive Doric columns and a ring of two steps, suggestive of a baptismal pool. This space is empty, low and dark. As we pass through to the burial chamber itself, our eyes are drawn up by the sudden height and dazzling patterns of sunlight filtered through amber glass. Only here is the symbolism of death apparent: sarcophagi; snakes, which shed their skin as the soul sheds its body; and angels in the vault.

The Mausoleum – exterior. Photo: Martin Charles

The Mausoleum – interior. Photo: Martin Charles

# Additions to the Soane Gallery, 1817–1952

Soane's five rooms were always impossibly crowded with paintings. Subsequent donations – for instance of nine paintings from William Linley in 1835 and forty from Charles Fairfax Murray in 1911 – made the problem worse. It must have been obvious even as the Gallery opened to the public that it would have to find more wall space.

It is not surprising therefore that in the 1880s the almshouses were converted for Gallery use and between 1909 and 1939 five new galleries were added across the east front. While the almshouse conversion did not in any way affect the exterior view of the Soane building, the extension eastwards did. The architect, E. S. Hall, decided to cover Soane's arches with sympathetic but radically different forms. The Gallery's original appearance was further disguised when six windows were cut in the east facade in the 1950s. During the 1999 – 2000 refurbishment these windows were blocked off and Soane's design of arches was restored.

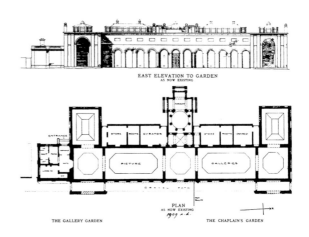

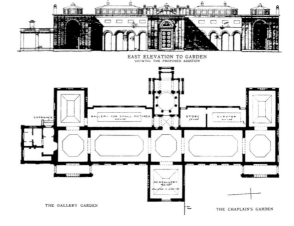

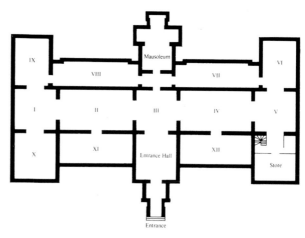

top:
E. Stanley Hall
*The East Front and Plan of the Picture Gallery 'as now existing' 1909*
Dulwich College Archive

middle:
E. Stanley Hall
*The East Front and Plan of the Picture Gallery 'showing the proposed addition', 1909*
Dulwich College Archive

bottom:
*Plan of the Picture Gallery when it re-opened in 1953*

# Rick Mather's 1999 Extension

During the same 1999–2000 project the architect, Rick Mather, sited a small extension with visitor facilities along College Road, to revive Soane's intention that the Gallery should be part of a second quadrangle.

The idea of the collegiate quadrangle and a subtle awareness of the site is particularly expressed by Rick Mather's bronze and glass 'cloister' running around two sides of the new quadrangle, linking every part of the old and the new buildings. The paired bronze fins of the cloister take their inspiration from the buttresses of the College Chapel, while elsewhere their spacing varies to reflect the different character of the building behind. These fins act as a support for the sunshade, a function which is reflected in their novel ladder-like form.

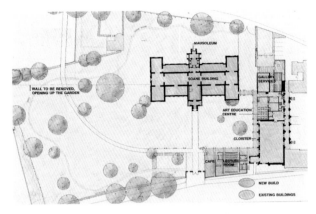

**Rick Mather Architects** *Proposed Ground Plan* 1996
Dulwich Picture Gallery, Archive

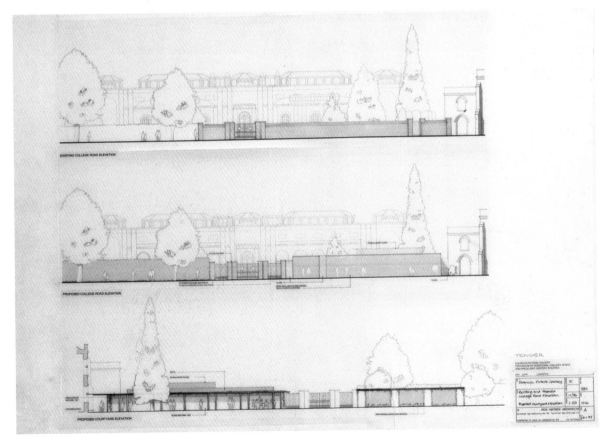

**Thomas Coward** for Rick Mather Architects *Existing and Proposed College Road Elevation* 10 January 1997
Dulwich Picture Gallery, Archive

View of enfilade after refurbishment and before picture hanging, April 2000
Photo: John Hammond

**Raphael**
*St Anthony of Padua*

# The Paintings

Dulwich Picture Gallery boasts one of the finest smaller collections of Old Masters in the world, full of household names and hidden gems. Bourgeois and Desenfans reflect the taste and market opportunities of their time by concentrating on European painting of the seventeenth and eighteenth centuries, the period sometimes known as the 'Age of Baroque'. Their taste was broad with a strong representation of all the major national styles of painting – Italian, Spanish, French, Flemish and Dutch. The great collection of English painting at Dulwich is largely due to two later donations. The group of Linley family portraits was given in 1835 and the Fairfax Murray Gift (also in the main comprising English portraits) in 1911.

European art has seldom been as rich as it was during the period 1600–1750; it has certainly never been as diverse. This was an age when artists working for radically different societies and did so with astonishing individualism and experimental audacity. The result is a dazzling range of styles and different ways of looking at the world.

To make sense of this kaleidoscope of painting, the collection has been hung by country and period. The Latins – the Italians, Spanish and French – are hung at the north end of the Gallery; the Northern Europeans – Flemish, Dutch and British – to the south (see plan on the inside cover).

The Gallery as a whole thus allows for a 'broad-brush' contrast between these two European polarities. For the Mediterranean cultures painting was primarily a public activity, used especially in the service of absolute princes and the Catholic Church. The inspiration of classical antiquity was particularly strong in these regions which lie at the very heart of the Roman Empire. The North Sea fringe of Europe, on the other hand, was also a fertile breeding ground for painters – especially the small but heavily populated area which embraces the low-countries (Flanders and Holland) and south

eastern England. These painters tended to work on a smaller scale, for a domestic market, concentrating on landscape and portraiture rather than religious painting.

Of course, no artist or country exactly fits this neat stereotype: Rubens, a Flemish painter, executed large-scale public religious works in the 'Italian' manner; many artists in the period from the north eastern part of France were physically and culturally much closer to their Flemish neighbours than to Italy. But there is a rough polarity of European painting in the period which can be felt if we compare an ideal Italian saint from one end of the Gallery with an all-too-real Flemish peasant from the other.

**David Teniers the younger**
*A Sow and her Litter* (detail)

# North End of the Gallery, Rooms 5, 6 and 13 – Italian Baroque Painting

Guido Reni's *St Sebastian* now hangs at the centre of the northern end of the Gallery as it did throughout the nineteenth century, the high altarpiece of Soane's interior. The Italian baroque paintings in the collection are hung around this historic centrepiece.

Guido Reni was revered in his own lifetime (and until the twentieth century) as the epitome of Italian art, with its respect for antique sculpture, its graceful figure drawing and its love of sensual beauty. These qualities can be seen throughout the Italian rooms: the compositions appear to be more designed than observed; they are dominated by sculptural figures put into athletic or expressive attitudes, with landscape (or indeed anything else) playing an insignificant part.

The Catholic church dominated Italian art during the period, as witnessed by the overwhelming preponderance of religious subjects on show. During its period of radical reform, know as the Counter-Reformation (*c.* 1550 – 1650), the Catholic church instructed painters to sell their message harder. Religious images were to be a Bible for the illiterate, telling their stories correctly, clearly and passionately. Italian baroque art makes demands on the emotions – with ecstatic saints, expiring martyrs and glimpses of glory.

The 'Baroque' refers to a style of painting, sculpture and architecture which evolved in Rome in the 1630s and gradually spread throughout Europe (especially in Catholic countries) during the period *c.* 1650 – 1750. It is best seen in the Dulwich collection in the work of Bellucci and Sebastiano Ricci. The Baroque is characterised by an instability of composition; a dynamism which seems to whip up every part of a painting; an expressive extravagance of gesture; flamboyant patterns of drapery; and a dramatic use of light. 'Rococo' is a word sometimes used to describe later baroque art, for example the works of Giovanni Battista Tiepolo (see P. 21); it differs from the Baroque only in its lighter, more decorative and festive character.

**Sebastiano Ricci** *The Resurrection*

**Antonio Bellucci** *Saint Sebastian tended by Irene*

**Guido Reni** *St Sebastian*

## Guido Reni (Italian, 1575–1642)
### St. John the Baptist in the Wilderness

Oil on canvas (225.4 × 162.2 cm).
Painted in Bologna around 1636

Guido Reni felt that the purpose of art was to show us a beauty more perfect than that we could ever hope to see in the real world. This almost naked young man is the embodiment of that ideal beauty. Reni has made a pattern out of his posture – with arms and legs alternately bent and extended. He has shaped his limbs with graceful sweeping lines. He has turned a boy into a Greek god.

But a painting must tell a story, as well as being merely beautiful. This requires character. John the Baptist was no male model; he was a hermit, living in the wilderness on a diet of locusts and honey, calling on all who would listen to repent their evil ways. Guido Reni has domesticated this saintly savage, but there is still about the figure a certain 'designer' wildness. His hair is long and shaggy; his chest is gaunt and his navel knotted like a tree-stump. The gaping mouth and hand pointing up to heaven convey the urgency in the 'voice of one crying in the wilderness'.

## Guercino (Italian, 1591–1666)

### *The Woman Taken in Adultery*

Oil on canvas (98.2 × 122.7 cm).

Painted in Bologna around 1621

You might think that the young have come to learn from their elders and betters. The old man to the right, with a head as wise and noble as a patriarch's, is convincing a small crowd with so many proofs that he counts them out on his fingers. But you would be wrong, for this is a Pharisee – specialist in ensnaring the spirit of love in the letter of the law. He has brought before Christ an adulteress, who, according to scripture, must be stoned to death. Christ upholds the Law, only adding 'let he who is without sin cast the first stone'. No one comes forward.

Guercino doesn't just show us the action; he pitches us into it. Unlike other artists, he paints the moment when the crowd is gathering in anger rather than dispersing in shame. We only see the figures from the elbows up and even then they barely squeeze into the frame. We rub shoulders with them, yet we can hardly make out their gestures and reactions. What is more, this is something happening now: the woman and soldier are in 'modern' (that is seventeenth-century) dress. It is more confusing to be a participant than an onlooker. But this is the point of the story: in the moment of jostle, anger and corrupt advocacy, there is a 'still, small voice of calm', a man who practises and teaches righteousness.

# Giovanni Battista Tiepolo (Venetian, 1696–1770)
## *Joseph Receiving Pharaoh's Ring*

Oil on canvas (106.1 × 179.7 cm).

Painted in Venice around 1735

Pharaoh hands Joseph a ring to show that he has chosen the young Jewish ex-slave as his second-in-command over all the land of Egypt. A tale of country-boy made good is given extra glamour by a foreign setting. There may even be some identification here between the artist and subject, as Tiepolo, like many clever Venetians during the eighteenth century, enjoyed his greatest triumphs abroad.

The Egypt of the Pharaohs is an excuse for an exotic fantasy. Spiky crowns perched on turbans; dragons crouching on helmets; black pages; bright silks, strangely slashed and crumpled; all these things suggest barbaric splendour. The same close-up effect which Guercino used for confusion, Tiepolo uses for wonderment. It is as if the eye cannot possibly absorb the full panorama of opulence. The royal palace and its staff of trumpeters, pages and guards can only be guessed at by fragments of figures, columns and balconies, glimpsed at odd angles, overlapping each other or cut off by the frame. There is a restless bombardment of the eye – the spaces between the principle figures offering more bizarre and attention-seeking incident than the figures themselves.

# Room 13 – Spanish Painting

Bourgeois and Desenfans, like most of their contemporaries, knew little about Spanish painting. There were however two artists who had been admired throughout Europe for a century or more – Velázquez (exclusively for his portraiture) and Murillo. Neither's work was thought of as particularly Spanish; instead it was admired for its cosmopolitan qualities: for its resemblance to Italian masters like Titian, and to Flemings like Rubens and Van Dyck, who worked in the Italian manner.

This is certainly an understandable view of Murillo's work. His *Madonna of the Rosary* of *c.* 1670 is an example of the sort of altarpiece produced throughout the Catholic world during the Counter Reformation. It depicts the vision of St Dominic in which the Virgin offers him a Rosary – a string of beads so called because St Dominic referred to it as 'Our Lady's crown of roses'.

The Rosary is a sort of abacus for counting out prayers to the Virgin and was believed to possess miraculous powers, particularly in combating heresy. St Dominic's vision has become our vision as the Virgin floats on clouds guided by angels and surrounded by golden light, smiling benignly down upon us, her worshippers.

Though Murillo's Madonna has so many affinities with Italian art and the work of Rubens and Van Dyck, his scenes of childhood (of which there are three magnificent examples in the collection) could not have been painted outside Spain. They have a truthfulness, an intense rendering of the feel and smell of real objects, and a melancholy which is peculiar to Spanish art. These qualities were not always appreciated: John Ruskin wrote of the Dulwich peasant boy scenes, 'Do not call this the painting of nature: it is mere delight in foulness'.

**Bartolomé Esteban Murillo**
*Invitation to the Game of Pelota*

**Bartolomé Esteban Murillo**
*Two Peasant Boys and a Negro Boy*

**Bartolomé Esteban Murillo** *The Madonna of the Rosary*

## Bartolomé Esteban Murillo (Spanish, 1617–1682)
### *The Flower Girl*

Oil on canvas (121.3 × 98.7 cm).

Painted in Seville around 1665

Hogarth once said that he had seen English cook-maids more beautiful than greek statues. Murillo here presents us with just such a below-stairs ideal. It is as if he is saying that an artist's skill lies not in inventing beauty but in recognising it in unlikely places. This peasant girl spreads open her shawl with an instinctive grace; her sleeves and head-scarf crumple rhythmically, like rose-petals. Reality is further sweetened by a downy surface and slight soft-focus, achieved by dragging thick paint lightly over a coarse weave of canvas.

But this is still earthly beauty; it could never be confused with Murillo's heavenly *Madonna of the Rosary* hung nearby. Even her smile is more mischievous than angelic. The cheap colours – oranges and browns – contrast with the costly blues and golds of the *Madonna*. A dull greyness lingers round the figure, as if ash had been mixed into the shadows. The drabness of this world is shown up by the radiance of the next. *The Flower Girl* is a meditation on transience – on a beauty as fragile as a plucked flower, threatened by a smoky dusk of decay.

# Room 4 – French Painting of the Seventeenth Century

This room is a show case for the great tradition of French classicism, seen more clearly here than anywhere else outside the Louvre. The founder of the style was Nicolas Poussin (1594–1665), who is represented by seven masterpieces. The man who did most to promote it was Poussin's disciple, the first President of the French Academy, Charles Le Brun (1619–90), who is represented by two.

The paintings in this room may seem quintessentially French but they really owe more to Rome than to Paris. Many of the artists – Claude, Poussin, his brother-in-law, Gaspard Dughet – spent their entire careers in Rome. Others made formative visits: Sébastien Bourdon in 1634–37; Swanevelt in 1624–41; Le Brun in 1642–5, when he studied Poussin's work and painted his *Horatius Cocles Defending the Bridge*. Yet these French *émigrés* painted in quite a different way from their Italian colleagues. The Italians revered the *spirit* of the antique, which they found as much in the works of Michelangelo and Raphael as in surviving Roman sculpture; Poussin studied the stones themselves, to learn a new way of composing paintings. Both Poussin and Le Brun were concerned with story-telling, not as a general evocation of a mood, but as a specific series of linked actions and states of mind. Their paintings demand to be read as well as looked at.

All the artists in this room were interested in landscape, something most Italians ignored. Poussin and Claude sketched together out of doors in the countryside around Rome. Their observation of nature was acute, especially their ability to record effects of light and air. They and their followers also appreciated that ancient civilisations had left such a deep footprint in this terrain, most obviously through architecture, that its overgrown ruins and ancient buried terraces could be used by landscape painters to tell a story, or at least to reinforce a dramatic mood. They invented something called 'classical' landscape painting, so called because it seemed to 'improve' nature – making it more ordered and dignified – in the way that classical sculpture 'improved' the human body.

**Charles Le Brun**
*Horatius Cocles Defending the Bridge*

**Nicolas Poussin** *Rinaldo and Armida*

## Nicolas Poussin (French working in Rome, 1594–1665)

### The Triumph of David

Oil on canvas (118.4 × 148.3 cm).

Painted in Rome around 1630

David returns in triumph with the giant Goliath's head on a pole to be fêted by the jubilant Israelites. The crowd here shares a single joy, but is made up of many different individuals and groups. We can learn much by examining their gestures and costumes. One man clenches his fist and points to his forehead to explain how and where David smote Goliath. Some young ladies to the left have patterned dresses and fussy hairstyles, clearly richer than the older women sitting on the floor with their children. Poussin records such distinctions of class to sharpen our awareness of the crux of the story. The hero is a mere shepherd-boy, with a short tunic and a skin bag. He lugs his own heavy trophy, more like a humble standard-bearer than a future king.

Poussin wanted his images to tell stories as precisely as a writer's words. To do this he evolved a new, more premeditated kind of painting. The composition seems to be made of stencilled or cut-out shapes; the drawing is sharp-edged; the surface is matt and evenly-finished. The figures have the same lucidity as the architectural background. The whole painting appears as though it has been chiselled out of stone.

## Nicolas Poussin (French working in Rome, 1594 – 1665)
### *The Nurture of Jupiter*

Oil on canvas (96.2 × 119.6 cm).

Painted in Rome around 1635

The baby Jupiter, threatened by his jealous father Saturn, has been smuggled to safety on the island of Crete. The future king of the gods is fed goat's milk and a wild honey-comb, cut from a tree on the open hillside. This is a pagan midsummer version of the Christmas story. The events take place during the Age of Saturn: a time not of barbarism but of peace and plenty, when food was there for the taking and when River Gods could still be seen reclining by their springs and tilting their urns.

As in the Triumph of David, Poussin paints like a carver. The standing Nymph in particular recalls antique stone reliefs, where figures are seen in strict profile with their drapery fanning out like a shell. But Poussin never forgets those parts of painting which sculpture lacks – colour and shading. Here, the principal figures are made to appear closer to the viewer and more prominent by strengthening the intensity of their colour and the contrast between their lit and shaded sides. The light of a hot dusty evening is conveyed by deliberately restricting the colours (especially in the landscape) to a narrow range of pastel pinks and blues. No artist can better suggest the qualities of a Mediterranean evening – the clarity of the strong sun-light and the heavy smell of the air.

## Claude Gellée, known as Claude Lorrain (French working in Rome, 1600 – 82)

### *Jacob and Laban, with his Daughters, Leah and Rachel*

Oil on canvas (72 × 94.5 cm).

Painted in Rome in 1676

Jacob has struck a bargain with his uncle: he will tend Laban's flocks for seven years in exchange for his younger daughter, Rachel. At the end of this time we see Laban fobbing him off with his first-born, Leah. Jacob will have to labour another seven years to earn his first choice of bride. Claude probably chose this episode from the Book of Genesis because it conveys a world of primitive nomads, where wealth is measured in livestock – a kind of Biblical Golden Age. The architectural forms are simple and pre-Classical – with squat towers and undecorated walls. Communication depends upon primitive vessels and half-hidden paths.

The village citadel nestles in the woods so that its outline is rounded and organic like an untouched hillside. The world is fresh and overgrown.

Claude excels in the depiction of air, especially the way in which it glows in the slanting sunlight at dawn and dusk. Leonardo da Vinci first observed that distances in landscape appear blue, especially at these times; Claude soaks the whole scene in this blue cast, as if every object, however close, is being looked at through a veil of coloured air. In this way he gives his landscape the sensation of space, but also an intangible, dream-like quality.

# Room 12 – 18th Century Painting in Europe

The diversity of European painting in the period 1600–1750 has already been remarked upon; it must be said however that regional differences diminish during the period. Anyone visiting the countries featured in the collection by 1750 would find far more common ground and interchange in the painting (and indeed the architecture) than they would have done a hundred years earlier. Room 12 celebrates this cosmopolitanism of eighteenth-century art.

Almost all the artists in this room travelled outside their native country. Claude-Joseph Vernet and Richard Wilson spent formative years in Rome. It had always been the way for northern artists to seek the artistic treasures of the south (as seen in Room 4); the eighteenth century saw a new species of migration – that of southern artists seeking the rich markets of the north. It was London, with its great wealth and meagre local artistic talent (at least until later in the century), which became the principal magnet for enterprising artists. Most of the continentals in this room visited London, either briefly, like Watteau, or for a protracted stay, like Canaletto, De Loutherbourg, Zuccarelli, Andrea Soldi and Sebastiano Ricci. The other English artists, Hogarth and Gainsborough, were comparatively insular (aggressively so in Hogarth's case), but even they were formed by London's cosmopolitan milieu. Hogarth was influenced by Watteau and the French Rococo; Gainsborough studied with the Frenchman, Gravelot, and was a close friend of De Loutherbourg, whose portrait he painted.

London had for centuries relied upon visitors for its best painters: one only has to think of Holbein, Van Dyck, Lely and Kneller. But never before had it been exposed to such a variety of styles and never before had it played a significant part in the cross-fertilisation of European painting.

**Francesco Zuccarelli**
*Landscape with a Fountain,*
*Figures and Animals*

**Andrea Soldi** *Louis Francois Roubiliac*

## Antoine Watteau (French, 1684–1721)
### *Les Plaisirs du Bal*

Oil on canvas (52.6 × 65.4 cm).

Painted in Paris around 1715

This is a scene of wish-fulfilment – a warm dusk in the marble-vaulted summer-house of an Italian garden. There is music from a rustic band, dancing in fancy-dress, romance, flirtation and chat. Watteau provides a glimpse of Earthly Paradise for the urbane. To the eighteenth-century viewer this scene would have appeared far more informal than it does to us. The outdoor setting, the mix of high and low life, the confusion of dressing up and dressing down; all these would have seemed a daring relaxation of etiquette. After the stuffiness of the Court at Versailles, this scene would have conveyed the idea of liberty. As the masked revellers sing in a similar scene from Mozart's *Don Giovanni*: 'Viva la Libertà.'

What makes the mood so vivid is Watteau's ability to suggest atmosphere, as if he is not just painting the figures, trees and columns, but also the light falling on them and the air surrounding them. He also understands the effect of a suggestive use of the paint brush. Much of the detail is sharp and sparklingly precise, but there are areas, particularly in the distance, where the touches become mysterious and open-ended to convey a confusion of leaves, sky and distant hills, seen through the falling waters of the fountain. John Constable thought this painting seemed to have been 'painted in honey: so mellow, so tender, so soft and so delicious'.

## Canaletto (Venetian, 1697–1768)
### *Old Walton Bridge*
Oil on canvas (48.8 × 76.7 cm).
Painted in London in 1754

Canaletto is best-known for his sparkling views of Venice, done for the tourist market, but here, and in vivid contrast to the Watteau, Canaletto's view is a matter-of-fact record of modern life in the Home Counties of England. The bridge over the river Thames at Walton had been constructed four years before this painting, to a daringly high-tech design. A coach crosses it; a boat lowers its mast to pass underneath the span. Thomas Hollis, the Whig MP who ordered the painting, has himself included in the foreground, along with a friend, a servant and a dog. This is a portrait of a specific person and a specific place; Canaletto even inserts himself as the artist on the stool, faithfully recording what is in front of him.

But Canaletto finds more in England than an efficient infrastructure. The dark green of the ground, the complex grey cloud-mass with evening light breaking across it; these subtly-observed effects convey exactly the smell of damp grass in the air during a changeable English summer. The atmosphere is heavy, but the touch is light and decorative, the paint forming tiny blobs and trails like Murano glass.

**Canaletto**
*The Bucintoro at the Molo
on Ascension Day*

# Room 2 – Flemish Painting of the Seventeenth Century

Flemish and Dutch societies were in dramatic contrast in the seventeenth century: Flanders was a Catholic part of the Hapsburg Empire, Holland an independent, Protestant republic. Until 1648, the two were almost continually at war. These differences had a clear impact on the type of paintings produced in each country.

During the Protestant revolt, 1568–1648, churches throughout Flanders had been ransacked by iconoclastic mobs. When re-conquered by Catholic forces these churches, and many newly built ones, required redecoration with large scale, public and emotive paintings. Flemish artists were commissioned by the Regents of the Spanish Crown in Brussels (and by their allies in the other Catholic courts of Europe) to produce similarly rhetorical (even propagandist) images for their palaces and triumphal processions.

The sheer scale of production on the part of Flemish artists, and the extent of their influence, can be guessed at by Rubens's oil sketches in this room, variously executed for an ambitious decorative scheme for a church, two over-life-size altarpieces (one in Antwerp and another in Genoa), a set of tapestries, and a group of large paintings given to Philip IV of Spain. Van Dyck's international impact is scarcely less remarkable: he worked extensively in Flanders, Italy and England and his portraits were the most sought after in Europe.

The Flemish were also well known as painters of landscape and peasant subjects, a type of painting invented by Pieter Breughel (active 1550–69) and represented in this room by an important group of paintings by David Teniers the Younger (1610–90). These pictures provide a comprehensive picture of the daily life of the times.

**Rubens**
*Venus Mourning Adonis*

**David Teniers the younger** *A Winter Scene with a Man Killing a Pig*

# Peter Paul Rubens (Flemish, 1577 – 1640)
## *St Barbara Fleeing from her Father*

Oil on oak panel (30.9 × 24.4 cm).

Painted in Antwerp 1620

In his later life, rather than working from drawings, Rubens used oil-sketches like this one as his preparation for a major painting. In this rapid first draft, a maximum of effect is created by a minimum of means. The panel is scrubbed with a buff-brown colour, over which the objects are floated in a paint layer so thin that the underpaint everywhere shows through. It is as if the figures are discovered in the brown ground, rather than drawn over it. A unified and luminous effect is achieved by a very narrow range of colours. There are two basic colour polarities – the brown of the under-paint and the faint grey of the clouds. In places the brown is heightened to red and the grey to a clear sky-blue. There are no unrelated colours.

Sketches like this were given to Rubens's pupils, who then worked them up into full-sized oil paintings. In this case the finished work hung on the ceiling of an aisle in the new Jesuit church in Antwerp, which is why the scene appears to be seen from below. It depicts St Barbara fleeing from her molesting father, who shut her up in the tower visible behind and subsequently killed her for her Christian faith. The colour harmonies tell the story: the father is red, hot and angry; St Barbara's swirling blue and white draperies look like clouds in the sky, a reference to the heavens to which she will soon ascend as a Holy Martyr.

## Peter Paul Rubens (Flemish, 1577 – 1640)
### Venus, Mars and Cupid

Oil on canvas (195.2 × 133 cm).
Painted in Antwerp 1630 – 35

Rubens felt that painters should imitate sculpture but not too closely. They should be particularly careful to record those creases, dimples and areas of fat which distinguish real bodies from cold marble. His Venus is a *painterly* nude: soft, fleshy, beautiful (though faintly imperfect), and boldly executed with a coarse brush. Rubens makes the viewer aware of the sense of touch, whether we are enjoying the real surface of the paint or the imaginary surface of the skin or armour.

But this painting is not merely sensual: Rubens wishes to flesh out his ideas. He uses Greek and Roman gods as the embodiments of abstract virtues, which might otherwise be impossible to visualise and to value. What at first seems to be a mythological family posing for their portrait, is in fact an allegory of the triumph of Peace over War, of Love over Hate. Mars (the God of War and appropriately set against a dark blood-red cloth) is literally disarmed by love: a little cherub cuts him from his armour. Venus meanwhile (the Goddess of Love and suitably light, white and tender) nourishes her baby, Cupid. The child clutches at his mother and is narrowly saved from falling. Below Cupid lies Mars's shield, with a monstrous face carved on it, like an evil black hole cut through the painting. The baby seems to be dangling over the mouth of Hell. To protect the spirit of love is a precarious venture, according to Rubens, especially at the height of the Thirty Years War.

## Sir Anthony van Dyck (Flemish working in Flanders, Italy and England, 1599–1641)
### *Venetia Stanley, Lady Digby, on her Death-bed*

Oil on canvas (74.3 × 81.8 cm).

Painted in England 1633

Venetia Stanley (1600–33) was famous for her dazzling beauty and notorious for the sexual licence of her youth, something not usually tolerated in English seventeenth-century high society. Sir Kenelm Digby, a poet and scientist of some distinction, fell so completely in love with her that in 1625 he married her, in secret and against the wishes of his family.

When Lady Digby died unexpectedly in her sleep, during the night of 30 April 1633, Sir Kenelm was so distraught that he summoned Van Dyck to record the transitory beauty of her corpse. Sir Kenelm later wrote that this 'is the Master peece of all the excellent ones that ever Sir Anthony Vandike made, who drew her the second day after she was dead; and hath expressed with admirable art every circumstance about her, as well as the exact manner of her lying, as for the likenesse of her face; and hath altered or added nothing about it, excepting onely a rose lying upon the hemme of the sheete, whose leaves being pulled from the stalke in the full beauty of it, and seeming to wither apace, even whiles you looke upon it, is a fitt Embleme to express the state her bodie then was in'.

In the posture and the patterns of bedding Van Dyck offers two consoling visual suggestions: that death is but sleep and that Venetia (or her soul) is floating on clouds surrounded by the blue skies of Heaven.

# Room 11 – Dutch Seventeenth-Century Painting

Dutch painting was quite unlike any other during the seventeenth century; but then so was Dutch society. In a Protestant Republic neither church nor court were important patrons of art. Instead, painters worked for a new and expanding middle class which had become spectacularly wealthy through Holland's maritime trade. These merchants (and the innkeepers, tradesmen and artisans who benefited from the general Dutch economic miracle) had relatively small town houses to decorate, and not much time for the complicated business of finding an artist and devising an appropriate commission, unless it was for a simple portrait. They bought their paintings 'off the peg' in dealers' shops, or even from stalls at fairs.

Dutch artists had to catch the eye of their public with small-scale paintings which were easy to appreciate. And the easiest thing to appreciate in painting is resemblance to nature – at which the Dutch excelled. They also became specialists: they honed their extraordinary technical skills to the depiction of one particular aspect of the world. In this room we can see examples of portraiture, landscape, sea-scape, city-scape, genre (the depiction of everyday life) and flowers; all specialist branches of painting which the Dutch carried to perfection (and many of which they invented). Religious and mythological paintings stand out here as oddities, just as landscapes and genre paintings would in the Italian room.

Dutch art appears to be a simple mirror. It is sometimes difficult to appreciate the invention as well as technical skill which goes into making images which remind us so powerfully of the world.

opposite page:
**Jan van Huysum**
*Vase with Flowers*

**Jan van der Heyden**
*Two Churches and
a Town Wall*

## Rembrandt van Rijn (Dutch, 1606 – 69)
### *Jacob III de Gheyn*

Oil on oak panel (29.9 × 24.9 cm).

Painted in Amsterdam in 1632

This portrait looks at first like the product of an unpromising commission. How could a painter be expected to make much of a single head on such a small scale, especially when his sitter insists on wearing such sober clothes? Rembrandt accepts that there is nothing much to be done compositionally: he even makes a virtue out of this simple, direct and frontal arrangement. But there are two other vital elements which he uses to infuse life into the image. The first is light. The cheek is so brilliantly lit that the detail appears to have been lost in the glare. A glowing aura surrounds the head like the rings of Saturn. There is no obvious wall or surface reflecting this light, which seems to have a substance of its own.

Rembrandt observes that paint has texture as well as colour, and that it can be used to create form by building up a crust, almost like plaster relief. The creases around the right eye are etched in the paint surface, as they were in De Gheyn's face.

# Rembrandt van Rijn (Dutch, 1606 – 69)
## *A Girl at a Window*

Oil on canvas (81.6 × 66 cm).

Painted in Amsterdam in 1645

One of the aims of painting is to deceive the eye: to make us believe, even for a second, that we see something that doesn't really exist. There is a more vivid sensation of reality – the eye is more cheated – in this painting than in any other in the Gallery. This effect is achieved by the use of texture. The paint layer is applied so thickly, so coarsely and with so much improvisation (using a palette-knife and fingers as well as brushes) that it almost *becomes* the plaster, the stone and the linen which it depicts. If we don't believe our eyes, we feel that we could reach out and touch these surfaces, each with their distinctive feel.

To bring reality within reach Rembrandt has pushed everything in the painting forward, so that the girl and the ledge upon which she leans seem to project out of the front of the frame. But Rembrandt is not interested in a simple trick of deception. On the one hand he offers solid reality; on the other he veils forms in mystery and uncertainty. The light is impossible: a bright pool covers the figure and the wall beside, leaving the top and the sides of the image swallowed up by darkness. Rembrandt has given his light unnatural properties in order that it can suggest things which lie beyond natural observation. The light here radiates from the figure like body heat. The analogy, which Rembrandt seems to be employing, between light and heat explains why the front few feet only of the scene are lit, for while we can see distant objects we can only feel warmth in close proximity. Without our being aware of the device, this pattern of light conveys to our subconscious the idea of moral or spiritual warmth.

## Gerrit Dou (Dutch, 1613 – 75)
### *A Woman Playing a Clavichord*

Oil on oak panel (37.7 × 29.8 cm).
Painted in Leiden 1660 – 5

In his life-time Dou's work was more valued than that of any other Dutch artist including his master Rembrandt. What his contemporaries admired was the almost miraculous depiction of minute detail. Recently, this type of craftsmanship has become less appreciated, because it is believed to be 'mechanical', no more than the result of patience and labour. But imagination and interpretation are as much required by an artist when he paints with a single hair as when he wields a two-foot brush. Dou has thought especially carefully about light and how it strikes different surfaces. It is absorbed by the girl's frizzy hair like a cloud; it makes a sheen on the silks and velvets; it picks up the weave of the tapestry; it glows on the wood of the viola da gamba; it sparkles on the bird-cage; it almost swallows up the flowers on the window. It is no surprise that the most famous painter of light, Vermeer, was inspired by this painting.

There is no obvious subject here; it is merely a depiction of everyday life. This means that the original viewer would have gazed at a familiar world and seen a familiar-looking girl gazing back. With no narrative to absorb her attention, the girl opens an ambiguous kind of dialogue with the viewer. We seem to have disturbed her playing. It has been suggested that the musical instruments here are symbolic of love: that the girl is inviting the viewer to strike up an amorous duet.

## Arent de Gelder (Dutch, 1645 – 1727)
### *Jacob's Dream*

Oil on canvas (66.7 × 56.9 cm).

Painted in Amsterdam 1710 – 5

Night fell as Jacob travelled from Beer-Sheba to Haran, so he lay his head on a stone and dreamed he saw a ladder from earth to Heaven with angels ascending and descending (*Genesis*, chapter 28, verses 10 – 12). There is a mix of the homely and heavenly in this Bible story which has always appealed to artists. Arent de Gelder, Rembrandt's last pupil, dwells on the homely side, recreating the scene in a literal-minded, almost comic way with details like the stone pillow, the rustic drinking flask and rough clothes, lovingly described. We see a tired traveller huddled in a corner, surrounded by thorny trees and a wide, dark and inhospitable landscape.

We are perhaps more aware of the dreamer than the dream. For De Gelder imagines the glory of Heaven as an effect of landscape. There is no procession of angels striding up and down; rather a burst of light in the top corner as if the moon is just breaking through the clouds. The only distinct angel (held steady by an awesome wing-span) is painted as a simple triangular shape made up of vertical streaks. It appears more like a veiled apparition than a heavenly body, as if this figure (and the vision as a whole) were just a trick of the light.

# Room 9 – Dutch Italianate Landscape Painting

Landscape painting as we understand it was invented during the century 1550–1650. It derived from two separate traditions, one mundane and the other idyllic. Some artists, from Medieval manuscript illuminators to Teniers and Hobbema (seen in Rooms 2 and 11), depicted what could be seen in the course of a few hours' walk from the centre of any town in northern Europe. For others landscape was more imaginative – a form of pastoral poetry, a way back to the idylls of Virgil and Theocritus and the mythical Golden Age of Arcadia.

The northern Europeans – French, Flemish and Dutch – excelled in both these traditions, the only difference between them being that those of the idyllic persuasion generally felt the need to make a trip to Rome. The most famous of these were the Frenchmen, Claude and Poussin (whose works can be seen in Room 4), but they were by no means alone. They were loosely associated with a thriving community of Dutch landscape painters in Rome, who formed themselves into a club called the *Bentveughels* or 'Birds of a Feather'. These same artists are now commonly referred to as 'Dutch Italianate' landscape painters and this room contains one of the best selections of their work anywhere.

A handful of Dutch Italianates executed mythological scenes; most however used their Italian experience to convey a sense of wonder and nostalgia more subtly through golden skies, ideal shepherds and glimpses of antique ruins. Some artists, like Cuyp and Wouwermans, even used the same quality of imagination to make northern scenery as grand, golden and poetic as the classic ground of the Mediterranean.

**Cornelis van Poelenburch**
*Landscape with Ruins and Figures*

**Nicolaes Berchem** *Roman Fountain with Cattle and Figures*

**Aelbert Cuyp** *A Road near a River*

## Adam Pynacker (Dutch 1620/1–1673)
### *Bridge in an Italian Landscape*
Oil on oak panel (43.8 × 52.7 cm).
Painted in Schiedam around 1653

This is a perfect example of the Dutch vision of Italy. It shows how carefully these artists observed the spectrum of coloured light which occurs in the clear skies of the Mediterranean: an intense yellow surrounding the setting sun, changing through white to an equally intense blue in the top right corner. The transition is imperceptible, the paint surface miraculously smooth, as if a sunset has been sealed in glass.

Evening light affects the way we see the earth as well as the sky, right up to the ground in front of our feet. Pynacker observes the way it picks out individual elements – the reeds, the bark and the fringes of the right-hand bushes – and sets them aglow as if on fire. No artist can suggest better than Pynacker the sensation of space, of the air circulating round every branch, and the thickness of the evening atmosphere, with its smell of dust and moisture.

Dutch painters saw the Italian landscape as heroic as well as idyllic. This is an ancient Roman bridge, noble even in decay; these shepherds are the descendants of those described by Virgil. Pynacker pays homage with a suitably abased view-point, looking dramatically up through the arch, the figures silhouetted against the sky.

## Aelbert Cuyp (Dutch, 1620 – 91)
### *Herdsmen with Cows*

Oil on canvas (99 × 144 cm).
Painted in Dordrecht around 1660

All landscape painters must to some extent choose between solid forms and light, between the earth and the sky. They must decide whether to concentrate on the weight and solidity of the ground itself, or on the light and air through which it is seen. Cuyp, even in his early, less italianate works, chooses sky. In *Herdsmen with Cows*, to give it due prominence he adopts the lowest possible view-point, so that even the nearby cows project above the horizon. Everything in the painting is affected by the quality of the light striking it. Even the weeds, stumps and grasses of the foreground are lit up in strange patterns by the slanting light of the setting sun. Beyond the foreground ridge, we have to peer through the glowing mist to make out the river and distant mountains.

Colour is again dictated by light, with the golds and blues of the sunset predominating over the greens and browns of the grass and the earth. There is a ring of coloured air surrounding the sun, almost like a rainbow, which extends over the earth as well as the sky. Cuyp learned these effects from Claude and from Dutch artists working in Rome. The setting here is not specific, but it is more Dutch than Italian. Cuyp wishes to show how light can transform even an ordinary, local scene.

**Aelbert Cuyp** *Landscape with Cattle and Figures, c.* 1640/1

# Room 10 –
# Painting in England in the Seventeenth Century

So far, every room has been dominated by paintings from the original Bourgeois Bequest; in this room there is only a handful of Bourgeois pictures. Here we see the paintings which were owned by Dulwich College before it dreamed of having a public gallery, and in particular those bequeathed in 1686 by the theatrical manager William Cartwright. His many portraits of family and acting friends and his odd landscapes, like Cornelis Bol's view of London, give a unique insight into the quality of art available in England at the time. It is this group of works which prompted the Pre-Raphaelite painter, Charles Fairfax Murray, to give to Dulwich in 1911 his collection of early English portraits, with their unusually strong representation of seventeenth-century masters.

It is obvious from the artists' names in this room that English painting in the seventeenth century was dominated by foreigners. This was nothing new: ever since Holbein became court painter to Henry the Eighth, the English aristocracy expected to import their best painters from the Continent. Van Dyck (whose English works may be seen in Room 2) created the image of the Court of Charles I; Sir Peter Lely did the same for Charles II. The other dominant visitor, Sir Godfrey Kneller, is represented in Room 3. Holbein and Kneller came from Germany; Van Dyck and Lely, and the vast majority of visiting artists during this period, came from the Low Countries. This room displays many lesser names who came to England from Flanders or Holland to take advantage of the same market – Gheerhaerts, Honthorst, Soest, Castro and Vanderbank. Indeed, so strong is the Netherlandish character of painting in England that we have been able to find a home in this room for some Dutch paintings with no English connections, knowing that they would not look out of place. In spite of the dominance of foreigners, the Cartwright and Murray collections do allow us to watch native artists beginning to find their feet. John Riley, Mary Beale, and Isaac Fuller are all important names in this early history of English painting, while John Greenhill is an accomplished artist whose works are really only known through the remarkable group here at Dulwich.

The problem with painting 'over here' is already clear to see – the average English patron wanted a handful of landscapes or seascapes (usually showing recognisable things or places) to accompany rooms full of portraits. Lely's *Nymphs by a Fountain* is a glorious but sadly rare exception to this rule.

**Cornelis Bol** *Westminster and the Thames*

British School (**Isaac Fuller**?) *Portrait of a Man (Self-Portrait?)*

## Sir Peter Lely (Dutch working in England, 1618–80)
### Nymphs by a Fountain
Oil on canvas (128.9 × 144.8 cm).

Painted in London around 1650

Lely always regretted the fact that he had so little opportunity to paint Arcadian scenes like this one. According to his poet friend, Richard Lovelace, England was an 'un-understanding land' where painting was concerned, with patrons only interested in adoring 'their own dull counterfeits'. In other words, the English only liked portraits.

This painting seems to show Lely working in the same tradition of history painting as Poussin's *The Nurture of Jupiter* (see p. 31), until we look closer at some of the details. For one thing the subject of Lely's painting is obscure or non-existent, apparently no more than an excuse to paint naked women. Moreover, there is something about the treatment of the figures which is disconcertingly immediate for a type of painting which is supposed to evoke the remote past of the poetic imagination. These nymphs have the hair-styles and the discarded clothes of the 1650s rather than of pre-history. Their bodies are not abstracted or idealised in the manner of antique sculpture. By seeking to tear off the idealising conventions which can seem to clothe the academic nude, Lely delivers the shock of real nakedness, rendering his nymphs less uplifting but more erotic.

# Rooms 1 and 3 –
# English painting in the Eighteenth century

**Joshua Reynolds and Studio** *Mrs Siddons as the Tragic Muse*

The founding bequest of 1811 included very few English paintings – only some portraits of Desenfans, Bourgeois and their friends and a group of six paintings by Reynolds. The Alleyn and Cartwright paintings (mostly English) still hung in the College when the Gallery opened in 1817. Early visitors must have received a clear message: only through the work of Sir Joshua Reynolds, the First President of the Royal Academy, could British art be considered to have come of age. The Reynolds which best expresses this conscious aspiration to go beyond the 'mere portrait' and to match the achievements of the old masters is his modern 're-staging' of a Michelangelo Sibyl – *Sarah Siddons as the Tragic Muse*. The first version of this painting (now in the Huntington Art Gallery, San Marino) so impressed Desenfans that he commissioned the replica which hangs in Room 3.

We have already seen in Room 10 that the Cartwright, Alleyn and Fairfax Murray paintings give an excellent account of painting in England during the seventeenth century. However the gift which did most to correct the Founders' high-minded dismissal of the art of their contemporaries in Britain was the bequest in 1835 by William Linley of nine family portraits. The Linleys were a distinguished family of musicians living in Bath who fortunately became friends of the most successful painter working there at the same time, Thomas Gainsborough. Add the magnificent full-length of Mrs Moody (given in 1831) and the Gallery possesses an unequalled group of Gainsboroughs which allows Room 1 to celebrate his art at the same time as commemorating the Linley family.

In Room 1 it becomes possible to enjoy in English painting some of the effects seen in the rest of the collection – a lightness and brilliance of brushwork, an animation of posture and a sense of mood or atmosphere which gives to the figures a suggestion of what we might now call an 'inner life'.

**Thomas Lawrence** *William Linley*

## Thomas Gainsborough (English, 1727 – 88)
### *The Linley Sisters*
Oil on canvas (199 × 153.1 cm).
Painted in Bath 1771 – 2

Elizabeth and Mary Linley were both professional singers; they were daughters of the composer, Tom Linley the Elder, and sisters of the most distinguished musician in the family, the composer and friend of Mozart, Tom Linley the Younger. Elizabeth (seen here standing) later married the playwright, Richard Brinsley Sheridan. This painting is more about their characters than their singing careers. They have sought out this secluded woody bank not just in order to practise, but because of their instinctive love of wild places. To love Nature was regarded in the eighteenth century as a virtue in itself and as a symptom of 'natural' fine feelings: the same feelings that lead these sisters to love each other. They exhibit what their contemporaries called 'sensibility'.

Though wearing silk gowns of the latest fashion, the sisters seems to blend with their woodland setting. Gainsborough echoes the colours of the landscape and even its rough texture in the painting of the costumes. Coarse grasses grow over Mary's dress almost as if they were being stitched into its design. More than anything it is Gainsborough's handling which lends the image its remarkable organic unity. He was famous for using long-handled brushes and for working up every part of the painting together. The brush-strokes are long, loose and capricious, more like the free shading of a rapid pen sketch than a finished painting.

**Thomas Gainsborough** *Thomas Linley the elder*

Published by Dulwich Picture Gallery, Gallery Road, London SE21 7AD

Designed by Herman Lelie
Typeset by Stefania Bonelli
Production co-ordinated by Uwe Kraus
Printed in Italy by Musumeci

ISBN 1 898519 14 5

British Library Cataloguing-in-Publication Data:
A catalogue record is available from the British Library